■ EASY START

The ice cream van

Series editor: Keith Gaines

Illustrated by Margaret de Souza

Nelson

Ting, ting.
Ting, ting.

"It's the ice cream van,"
said Kim's Mum.
"Let's have an ice cream."

3

"Can I have a little pink one
please?" said Kim.

"Can I have a big brown one
please?" said Rob.

"I will have a little brown one please," said Kim's Dad.

"I will have a big pink one
please," said Kim's Mum.

Kim's Mum went to get

them from the ice cream van.

"There you are," she said.

"A big pink one for you, Rob ...

... a little brown one for you, Kim ...

... a big brown one for you,
Dad ...

... and a little pink one for me."

10

"No, it's a big brown one for Rob,"

said Kim,

"and a big pink one for you."

"It's a little brown one for Dad,
and a little pink one for me."